MIGHTY MACHINES IN ACTION

Ambulances

by Chris Bowman

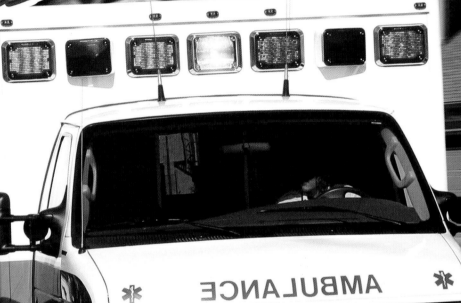

BLASTOFF! READERS 2

BELLWETHER MEDIA • MINNEAPOLIS, MN

Note to Librarians, Teachers, and Parents:

Blastoff! Readers are carefully developed by literacy experts and combine standards-based content with developmentally appropriate text.

Level 1 provides the most support through repetition of high-frequency words, light text, predictable sentence patterns, and strong visual support.

Level 2 offers early readers a bit more challenge through varied simple sentences, increased text load, and less repetition of high-frequency words.

Level 3 advances early-fluent readers toward fluency through increased text and concept load, less reliance on visuals, longer sentences, and more literary language.

Level 4 builds reading stamina by providing more text per page, increased use of punctuation, greater variation in sentence patterns, and increasingly challenging vocabulary.

Level 5 encourages children to move from "learning to read" to "reading to learn" by providing even more text, varied writing styles, and less familiar topics.

Whichever book is right for your reader, Blastoff! Readers are the perfect books to build confidence and encourage a love of reading that will last a lifetime!

This edition first published in 2018 by Bellwether Media, Inc.

No part of this publication may be reproduced in whole or in part without written permission of the publisher. For information regarding permission, write to Bellwether Media, Inc., Attention: Permissions Department, 5357 Penn Avenue South, Minneapolis, MN 55419.

Library of Congress Cataloging-in-Publication Data

Names: Bowman, Chris, 1990- author.
Title: Ambulances / by Chris Bowman.
Description: Minneapolis, MN : Bellwether Media, Inc., 2018. | Series: Blastoff! Readers: Mighty Machines in Action | Includes bibliographical references and index. | Audience: Ages 5-8. | Audience: K to Grade 3.
Identifiers: LCCN 2017031301 (print) | LCCN 2017032235 (ebook) | ISBN 9781626177567 (hardcover : alk. paper) | ISBN 9781681034614 (ebook)
Subjects: LCSH: Ambulances–Juvenile literature.
Classification: LCC TL235.8 (ebook) | LCC TL235.8 .B69 2018 (print) | DDC 629.222/34–dc23
LC record available at https://lccn.loc.gov/2017031301

Editor: Rebecca Sabelko   Designer: Steve Porter

Printed in the United States of America, North Mankato, MN.

Table of Contents

TO THE RESCUE!

Wee-woo! An ambulance's **siren** calls out as its lights flash. There is a crash!

siren

N.Y.

551

F.D.

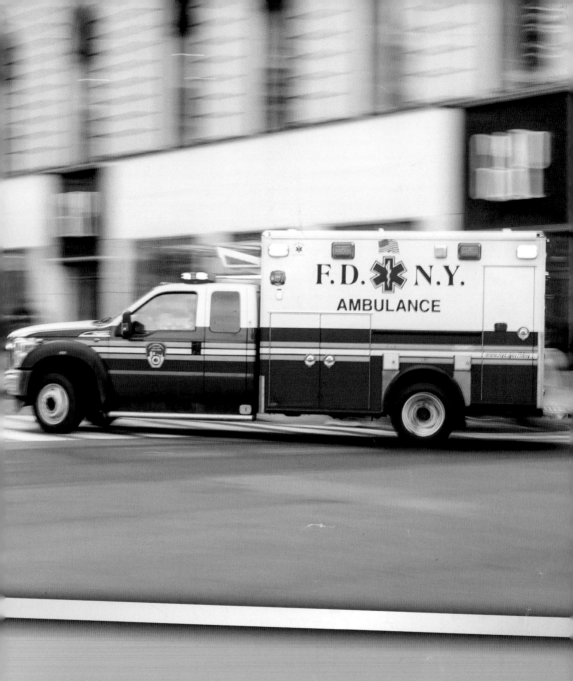

Cars move out of the way as the ambulance races down the street.

stretcher

Medics treat the man's **injuries**. They put him on a **stretcher** and load him into the ambulance.

It speeds to the **hospital**.
The man's life is saved!

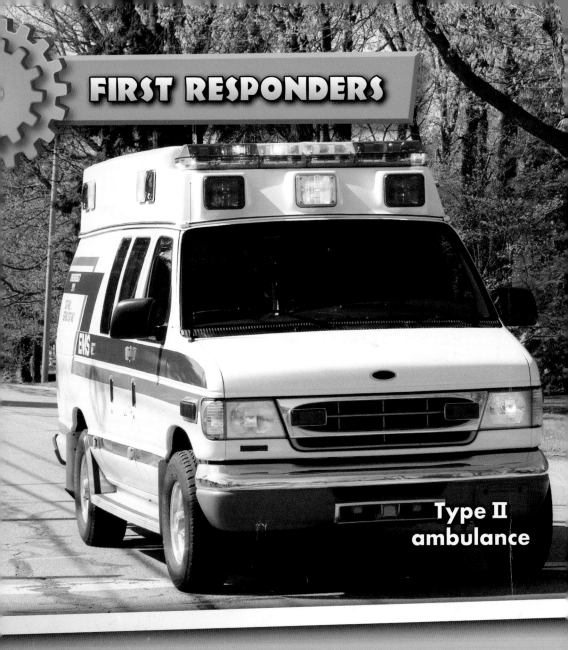

Type II ambulance

Ambulances help during **emergencies**. They carry supplies and sick or injured people.

These machines can be many shapes and sizes. They are found everywhere.

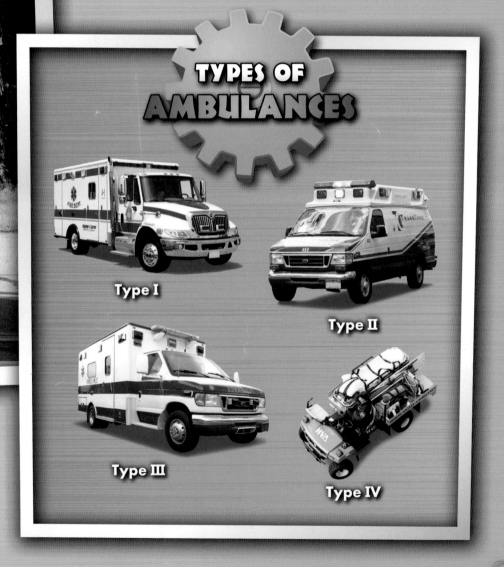

TYPES OF AMBULANCES

Type I

Type II

Type III

Type IV

Sometimes people need help where roads do not reach. Boat ambulances help during water emergencies.

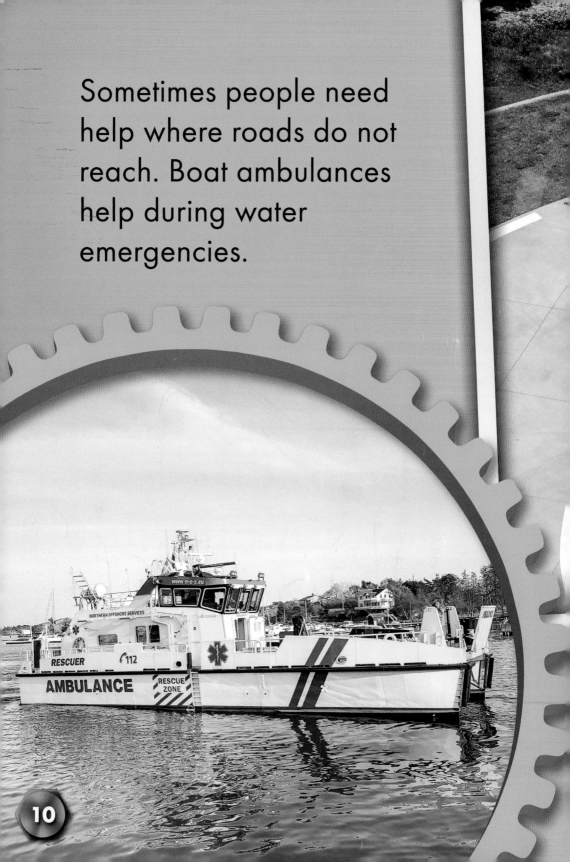

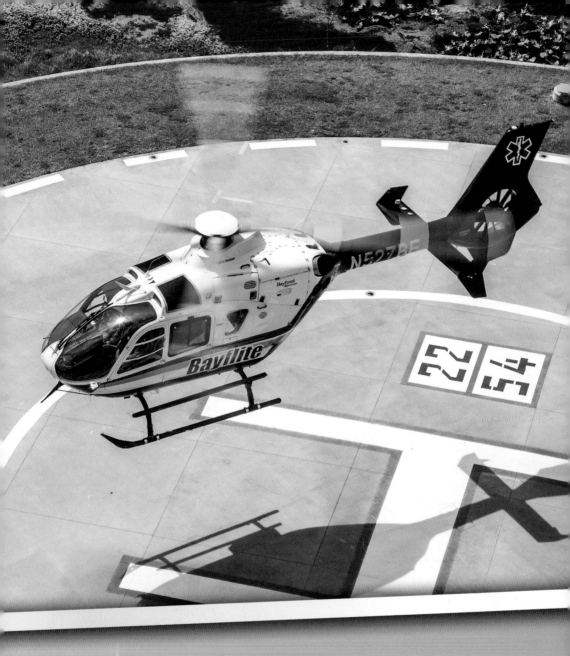

Helicopter ambulances fly to
mountaintops and deep forests.

ENGINES, SIRENS, AND GEAR

Powerful engines get ambulances to emergencies fast!

Type I
ambulance

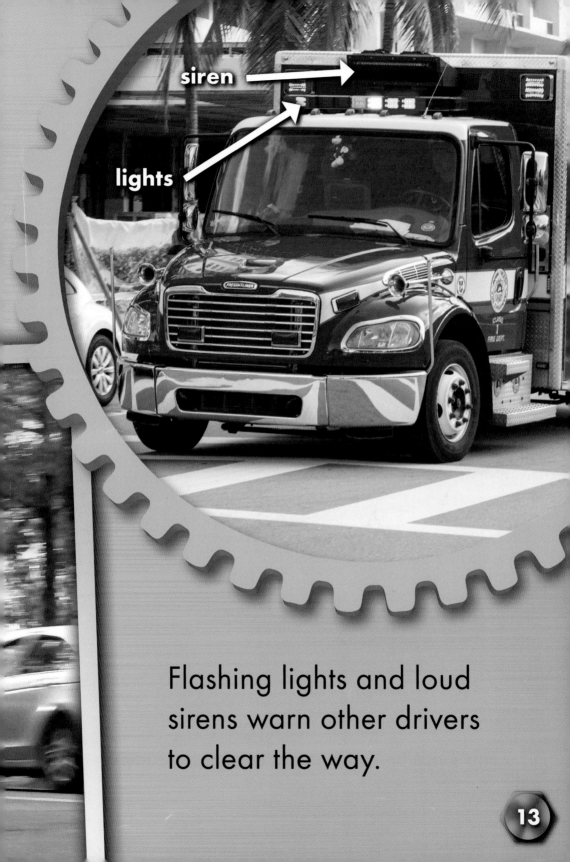

siren

lights

Flashing lights and loud sirens warn other drivers to clear the way.

Many ambulances have a lot of space.

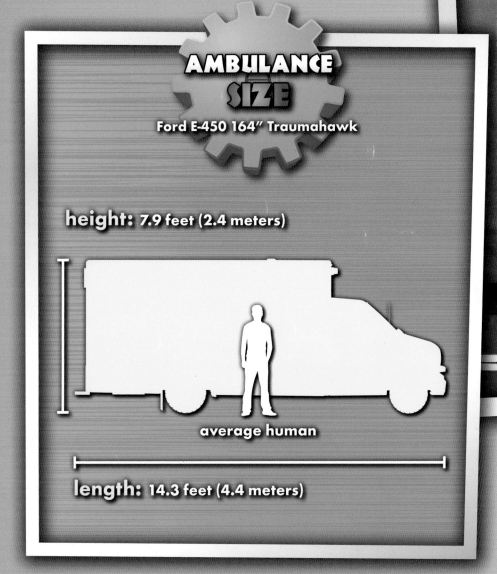

AMBULANCE SIZE

Ford E-450 164" Traumahawk

height: 7.9 feet (2.4 meters)

average human

length: 14.3 feet (4.4 meters)

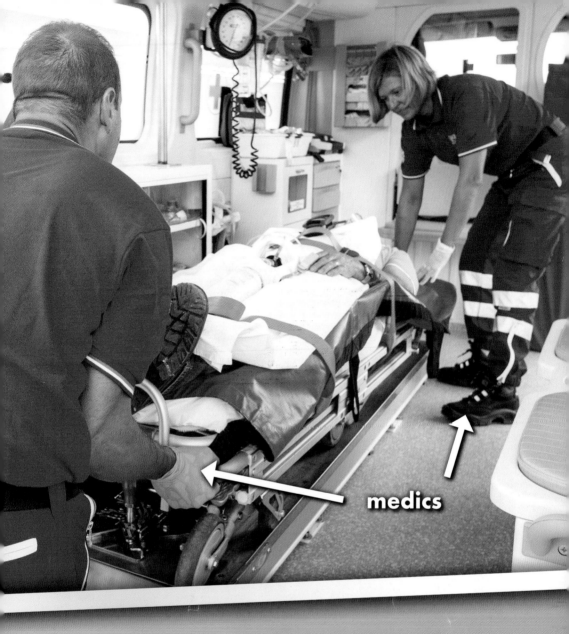

medics

There is room to store gear and **medicine**. High roofs allow medics to move around.

All ambulances have lifesaving supplies. They are ready for burns, broken bones, and heart attacks.

← **oxygen tanks**

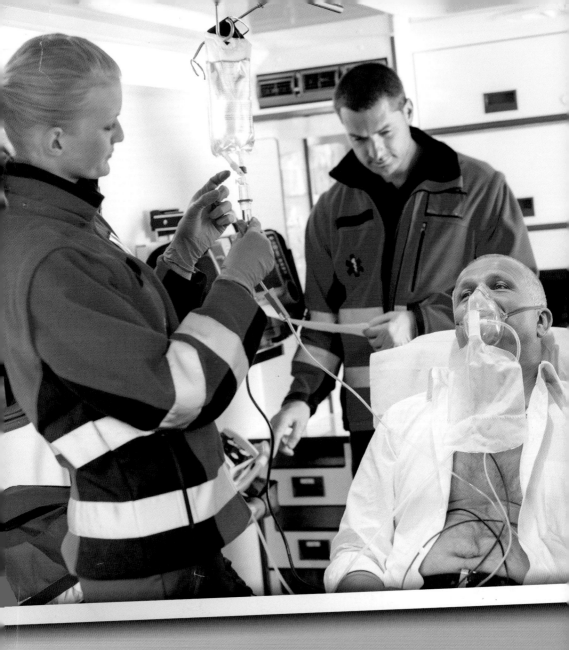

Onboard **oxygen tanks**
keep people breathing.

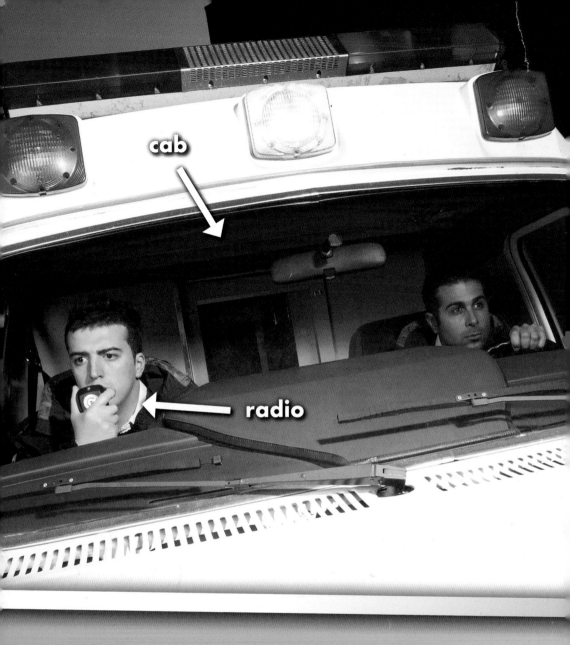

cab

radio

Ambulance drivers sit in a
cab. Radios keep them in
touch with hospitals.

Some cabs have a window behind the driver. This lets the medics share information.

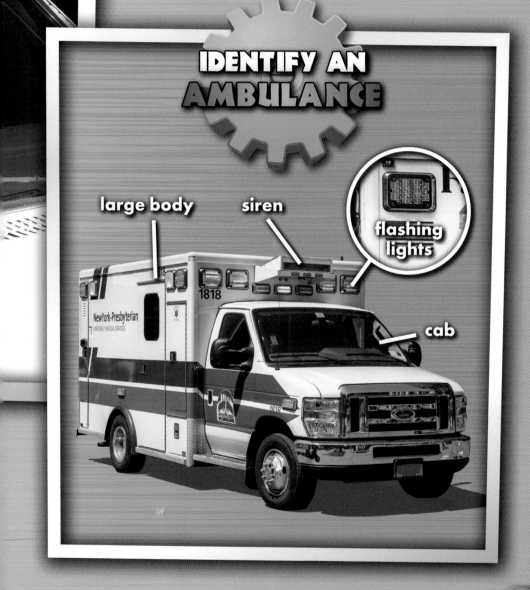

IDENTIFY AN AMBULANCE

large body

siren

flashing lights

cab

NewYork-Presbyterian
EMERGENCY MEDICAL SERVICES

1818

Ambulances speed to those who need help. They have the tools to care for the sick and injured.

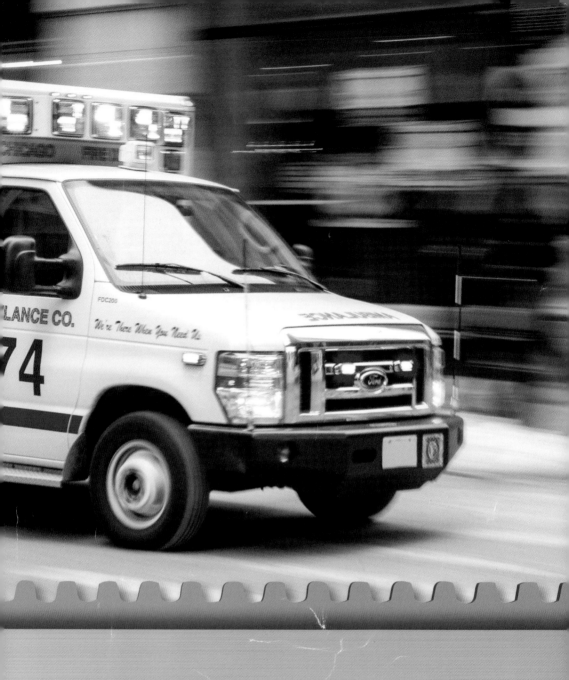

Ambulances and medics
truly are lifesavers!

Glossary

cab—the part of the ambulance where the driver sits

emergencies—serious and dangerous events that need quick attention

hospital—a building where doctors and nurses care for sick or injured people

injuries—pains or damages to the body

medicine—something used to treat pain or sickness

medics—people trained to treat sick or injured people

oxygen tanks—containers of air used to help people breathe

siren—an alarm that makes a loud sound to warn others

stretcher—a board used to carry sick or injured people

To Learn More

AT THE LIBRARY

Best, B.J. *Ambulances.* New York, N.Y.: Cavendish Square Publishing, 2018.

Graubart, Norman D. *Ambulances.* New York, N.Y.: PowerKids Press, 2015.

Staniford, Linda. *Ambulances to the Rescue Around the World.* Chicago, Ill.: Heinemann Raintree, 2016.

ON THE WEB

Learning more about ambulances is as easy as 1, 2, 3.

1. Go to www.factsurfer.com.

2. Enter "ambulances" into the search box.

3. Click the "Surf" button and you will see a list of related web sites.

With factsurfer.com, finding more information is just a click away.

Index

The images in this book are reproduced through the courtesy of: 2windspa, cover (Ambulance); romakoma, cover (Houses); Dan Callister/ Alamy, p. 4; Clari Massimiliano, pp. 4-5; Christopher Penler, pp. 6-7; Cathleen A Clapper, pp. 8-9; Chris Rabior 911 Images/ Alamy, p. 9 (Type IV); dov makabaw/ Alamy, pp. 9 (Type II), 13; Adolfolazo, p. 9 (Type III); Matthias Wolf, p. 9 (Type I); Drew Horne, pp. 10-11; Tommy Alven, p. 10; bakdc, pp. 12-13; William Perugini, pp. 14-15; CandyBox Images, pp. 16-17; Pavel L Photo and Video, p. 16; Radius/ SuperStock, pp. 18-19; dwphotos, p. 19 (lights); Giuliano Del Moretto, p. 19; Todd Bannor/ Alamy, pp. 20-21.

5